C000103722

EXPOSING THE HIDDEN CONNECTIONS OF FREEMASONS, THE CATHOLIC CHURCH, AND THE ILLUMINATI

James G. Battell

2023

CONTENTS

Some years ago during a trip to Cyprus, I happened to notice an English tourist, proudly wearing a Masonic medallion around his neck. I knew that I had to try and bravely engage this man and see what he truly knew about his religion, and of course witness to him as well. At first, he seemed ignorant of the fact that Freemasonry and Biblical Christianity are not remotely compatible with one another. This surprised him and caused him to become rather irate with me (he had stated to me how he was an Anglican). But persist I did, and before we parted from what was now becoming rather a hostile territory, I told him that Albert Pike, one of his religion's most cherished and trusted high priests, had put in print how Lucifer was the Masonic god which they actually worshipped (more on this later). He told me that he had never heard of Pike, which didn't surprise me too much, for he was only a third-degree freemason, but it was obvious to me that he believed my facts to be completely wrong.

I continued to explain why he needed to exit freemasonry and receive Jesus Christ as his own personal Saviour, but I could tell he really wasn't interested, as he sipped on his beer while his wife looked on with irritation towards me. And I later heard him telling his wife how I had called him a Satanist, which I hadn't. Of course, indirectly, he was worshipping Satan, as are all people before they receive Christ as their Lord and Saviour.

But when it comes to researching freemasonry or even being able to speak to members of this hand-picked private religion for those with money and power, such will tell you that they are not a "secret society" and are now "very open and transparent." That, of course, is far from the truth and not even remotely honest, for they will not allow cameras inside their lodges to film their religious services, nor will they allow their macabre rituals to be aired online or on air for all to see.

In fact, their religion is so secretive and selective, that Freemasons are unable and unwilling to share their religion in public, distribute pamphlets or DVDs to passersby, or warn people that the penalty of being a non-Mason will result in spending eternity in Masonic hell! The point being, they have no good news for non-freemasons and no warning or penalty for non-freemasons. It's simply a repackaged Babylonian humanistic deistic religious set-up!

For those that know next to nothing about the Freemasons, the Catholic church, the Illuminati and their hidden associates and comrades, I believe this book will expose Freemasonry for what it really is – evil from top to bottom – and may God Almighty use this publication to help free Freemasons and others trapped in its clutches.

Cardinal John O'Connor flanked by two freemasons in his New York cathedral. All looks very cosy and ecumenical!

Author Michael Bradley shares my thoughts on the evil and deceptive ecumenical movement, and so I strongly suggest right from the outset: would it not just be wise to leave and forsake all such groups and groups within groups and just follow the Lord Jesus Christ?

"...by the mid-eighteenth century the Masons, Rosicrucians, and other orders with professed Templar origins had become so entwined that it is hard for the modern historian to tell them apart" (ref. 13, p. 123).

Most freemasons and others in secret societies have no idea what they are involved in. I pray the Lord God of the Holy Bible will open their ears, souls, and minds to the truth found in the Lord Jesus Christ and the Holy Bible! Amen and amen.

WHEN DID FREEMASONRY BEGIN?

Freemasons teach that masonry was conceived during King Solomon's reign but they have to admit that this is loosely based only on their own private "tradition," which cannot be proven. Historians, actually date freemasonry to around 1717 AD (ref. 7, pg. 7).

Ever since its conception, Freemasons have tried to convince their critics that it isn't a religion, but more like a professional boys and girls club. (Yes women have their own lodge too. More on this later). However, because all freemasons are expected to believe in a god, or as they call him, "the Great Architect of the Universe," would it not at least be fair and accurate to at best categorise them as theists or deists and certainly not atheists?

It must also be noted that in 1847, the French freemasons allowed French lodge admittance to those that didn't believe in a god. However, British and American Freemasons were furious with this, so all formal ties were severed (ref. 10, p. 256-257).

IS FREEMASONRY A RELIGION?

According to Webster's Dictionary, freemasonry qualifies to be classified as a religion because they believe in a divine or superhuman power.... "to be obeyed and worshipped as the Creator and ruler of the universe, and this belief is conduct and ritual" (ref. 7, p. 12).

Typical modern humanistic claptrap

To affirm that Freemasonry is indeed considered a religion, may I quote the following Masonic sources: "Every Masonic Lodge is a Temple of Religion and its teachings are instruction in religion," Albert Pike (ref. 3, p. 4).

After Albert Pike, Albert Mackey is considered the most prominent of all Masonic leaders and writers.

Here he speaks about his religion: "Masonry is.....an eminently religious institution," Dr Albert Mackey (ref. 3, p. 4).

".....It is a religion without a creed, being of no sect but finding truth in all," Dr Albert Mackey (ref. 7, p. 7).

"Freemasonry certainly requires a belief in the existence of, and man's dependence upon, a Supreme Being to whom he is responsible" (ref. 7, p. 13).

"Masonry.....is a form of worship in which all religions can unite...", Sir John Cockburn, past deputy grand master of South Australia (ref. 3, p. 4).

This last quote would be music to the ears of the Roman Catholic-led and controlled ecumenical movement (called "churches together" in the UK). What Pope John XXIII couldn't initially achieve on his own during the 1960s, the freemasons and subsequent popes have helped him to finish. And how interesting it is that Masonic rituals are the same all over the world, much like the Catholic mass! Vain repetitions and carbon copy church rituals are condemned in Scripture (Matthew 6:7).

Former worshipful Masonic master, Jack Harris, said the following: "In other states [in the US]....the principle and the doctrines [of the ritual] are exactly the same. The wording only varies slightly" (ref. 7, p. 8).

Freemason, A. B. Grosh echoes this: "Judaism, Christianity, Mohammedanism recognize the only living true God; followers of different teachers, ye are worshippers of one God who is Father of all, and therefore, ye are brethren" (ref. 8, p. 7).

This quote, which dates back before the Second Vatican Council of the 1960s, is almost the same word-for-word statement from the above Masonic one, but it is in fact from the official Catholic catechism, of 1994: "The plan of salvation also includes those who acknowledge the Creator, in the first place amongst whom are the Muslims; these profess to hold the faith of Abraham, and together with us they adore the one, merciful God, mankind's judge on the last day" (Catechism of the Catholic church, p. 195).

Did you notice anything? The Lord Jesus Christ wasn't mentioned once!
Rome, which claims to speak with divine and infallible authority from "the seat of Peter," conveniently forgot to mention: "Neither is there salvation in any other: for there is none other name under heaven given among men, whereby we must be saved" (Acts 4:12).

During the 1960s, when cardinal John Heenan was England's most senior priest, the matter arose of a freemason wanting to convert to Catholicism, but retain his membership with them: "The Cardinal then took up the cause of 'regular' Freemasonry with Pope Paul VI. By 1971 he was able to report some progress. He told Carr of the recent case of a London Protestant who had married a Catholic woman. He now wished to become a Catholic but did not want to give up Freemasonry. Heenan sought guidance from the Holy See and was told the husband could become a Catholic 'without restriction.' This meant he could remain a Mason and take Communion [the Catholic Eucharist]. He entered the faith and even persuaded one of his Masonic brothers to follow his example" (ref. 15, p. 153-154).

This would certainly explain how the late Silvio Berlusconi and Tony Blair and other wealthy and powerful people were able to enjoy the best of both worlds!

Every lodge is designed to cater to "Christians," Muslims, Buddhists, and Jews. Freemasonry is very much an interfaith and ecumenical religion. This is one of the reasons why political parties in the west, and especially in the UK, are all very much the same today. They no longer have any visible or credible distinctions.

Should any professing Christian believe that Freemasonry is compatible with Biblical Christianity, please see the following quote: "A Christian Mason is not permitted to introduce his own peculiar opinions with regard to Christ's mediatorial office into the lodge" (ref. 3, p. 7).

The late Christian author Mr McCormick offers his thoughts to this stern rebuke to the "Christian" freemason: "Freemasonry is a religion without the

Holy Spirit. When the Lord Jesus Christ is denied as Saviour and Lord, the Holy Spirit (the Spirit of Christ) is absent. The Spirit may be mentioned occasionally but that certainly does not guarantee His presence or blessing. Remember! Only the Holy Spirit, through faith in the blood of Christ, can regenerate the soul" (ref. 3, p. 7).

(More on this later).

While some might wish to boast and applaud the Freemasons and the Rotary Club for all the good works they do, like collecting money for hospitals and other charitable deeds, one mustn't neglect the fact that, while good works are to be commended, they don't save the sinner from their sins. Only faith in the Lord Jesus Christ alone saves. Once a sinner is saved, the good should follow. But works without faith in Christ are pointless and vain (Romans 10:1-4).

THE MOST INFAMOUS FREEMASON

Albert Pike was a journalist, linguist, top lawyer, and thirty-third-degree sovereign grand commander of Scottish rite masonry. How they love their lavish titles (ref. 1).

Albert Pike proudly displays his thirty-third-degree Masonic regalia

In his infamous occult book, Morals and Dogma, he offers the following quote, which no doubt has haunted ex-freemasons, especially those that have come to Christ, for it makes it very clear who Freemasons actually worship. But please remember, this was only to be shared with those of the "higher degrees," a kind of "need-to-know" basis for the "privileged" and "enlightened" ones: "Masonry, like all the religions, all the Mysteries, Hermeticism and Alchemy conceals its secrets from all except the Adepts and Sages, or the elect, and uses false explanations and misinterpretations of its symbols to mislead those who deserve to be misled: to conceal the Truth, which it calls light, from them and to draw them away from it" (ref. 3, p. 11).

The following quote is even more controversial and has been accepted by some as being authentic (ref. 11), while others dismiss it (ref. 3).

I will share this quote and invite the reader to do further research into this whole murky and muddled subject: "The Masonic Religion should be, by all of us initiates of the high degree, maintained in the purity of the Luciferian doctrine. If Lucifer were not God, would Adonai whose deeds prove his cruelty, perfidy, and hatred of man, barbarism and repulsion for science, would Adonai and his priests calumniate him? Yes, Lucifer is God, and unfortunately, Adonai is also god...thus the doctrine of Satanism is a heresy; and the true and pure philosophical religion is the belief in Lucifer, the equal of Adonai; but Lucifer, God of Light and God of Good, is struggling for humanity against Adonai, the God of Darkness and Evil" (quoted by A.C. De La Rive in 'La Femme et l' Enfant dans la Franc-Maconnerie Universelle, 1889, p. 588).

William Schnoebelen, a former thirty-second-degree freemason, offers his sentiments on Pike and his "interest" in Lucifer: "He was also the Sovereign Pontiff of Lucifer...Pike chose to follow the mystery religions of Ba'al, he turned his back on God. If we look at his writings and statements attributed to him, we find that he acknowledged Lucifer as the true god and Adonai (the Biblical God) as the god of evil" (ref. 11, p. 191).

I would also like to produce another quote, this time taken by a close Masonic associate of Pike's, the thirty-third-degree Domenico Margiotta: "...With Lucifer the God of Light and Goodness struggling for humanity against Adonai the God of the Darkness and Evil...The Great Architect of the Universe is not the God worshipped by the Christians" (ref. 11, p. 193).

Freemasons take great delight in stating that only one in ten Masons know who Pike is, let alone read his books. And this was affirmed when The John Ankerberg Show wrote to fifty grand lodges in the US, seeking information as to which author they considered to be the most prominent, and the results came back as follows:

44% recommended Coil's Masonic Encyclopaedia by Henry Coil
36% recommended The Builders by Joseph Fort Newton
32% recommended Mackey's Revised Encyclopaedia of Freemasonry
16% recommended Morals and Dogma by Albert Pike (ref. 7, p. 9).

However, the following Freemason states just how

vast Pike's influence was: "Pike was a giant of his time who did extraordinary things in his lifetime. He was, in fact, the only Confederate soldier to be honored in America's capital: Washington, DC, where a huge statue of him dominates a major intersection" (ref. 1).

A special permit was given by Congress to allow Albert Pike to be buried in Washington DC.

I have seen this for myself when I visited Washington before I was saved. It is quite impressive for the unregenerate to glory in.

Or as one writer put it: "Albert Pike is to Freemasonry what Shakespeare is to drama."

And another: "He is the Plato of Freemasonry."

Freemasons also have a strange and blasphemous belief in that they and they alone know "the true name" of God, that being, they believe – JAH-BUL-ON.

This three-headed deity is meant to be Jehovah/Baal/Osiris all rolled into one!

(Incidentally, when Freemasons are asked whether this is true, they will lie and say it isn't or pretend they don't understand what you are talking about. They behave like shady politicians by invading the question).

This tactic is something all false religions and cults are very good at doing. But to the persistent and faithful researcher of Satanic religions, their perseverance sees right through such depravity and dishonesty.

Former US First Lady and spiritualist
Eleanor Roosevelt with a suspicious hand
symbol for those "enlightened" to spot

Two individuals with Masonic relatives have told me that they were scoffed at when asked about this odd title for the Masonic god. And even Charles Finney (once a Freemason himself) affirms this in his book: "Hence, if they are asked if the books in which Masonry have been published are true, they will either evade the question or else they will lie, and they are under oath to do so" (ref. 15, p. 12).

Only three Royal Arch Masons, when they kneel down together, with intertwined hands, under the royal arch, are allowed to whisper this "sacred" name.

This repulsive name-calling of God is so abhorrent to Bible-believing Christians that the following verse needs to be quoted: "That ye come not among these nations, these that remain among you; neither make mention of the name of their gods, nor cause to swear *by them*, neither serve them, nor bow yourselves unto them: But cleave unto the LORD your God, as ye have done unto this day" (Joshua 23:7-8).

Interestingly, the Vatican officially lifted the ban on its members being Freemasons in January 1983 (ref. 2, p. 104).

And a year later, the Church of Jesus Christ of Latter-day Saints "officially" allowed their members to become Freemasons. Of course Joseph Smith and Brigham Young had both been Freemasons all along, with other top-level Mormons: "...In 1984 the Grand Lodge of Utah made peace with the Mormons and today many Mormons are Freemasons" (ref. 10, p. 327).

Now, the interfaith/one-world religion can really get going (Revelation 18:4-8).

Adam Weishaupt, the son of a rabbi, later turned fundamentalist atheist (known in the Illuminati as "brother Spartacus") had also trained to be a Jesuit priest!

May 1 is their most important day of the year and it was this day that former British Prime Minister John Major, after an unprecedented <u>six</u>-week general election campaign in 1997, conveniently chose May 1 for voters to pick their next government.

May 1, 2003, George W. Bush decided to land a fighter jet on the USS Abraham Lincoln. After <u>six</u> hours on board, he told the world that all major hostilities in Iraq were now over.

Are these just coincidences or not? Or, was it a clear sign to the world that things were changing, i.e., world powers would launch pre-emptive strikes against sovereign states, new leaders would be elected to surrender more sovereignty to foreign powers; for was not Margaret Thatcher forced out of Downing Street by the Illuminati because she wouldn't go all the way when it came to surrendering more UK power to the EU? (ref. 13, p. 22).

Mr Bradley: "He [Weishaupt] studied the Masons and was later to form an alliance with them" (ref. 13, p. 64).

From its birth of only five members in 1776, yet ten years later, it was active and had gone global i.e., the US, Europe, and Africa.

According to Bradley, they used insider knowledge to control the UK stock market and took control of the Bank of England in 1785, when Napoleon was fighting Wellington.

He goes on to say that by 1818, they took control of the French economy, then the German economy. As Britain, Europe, and America backed both sides during the Iran/Iraq war in the 1980s, by providing them with weapons to kill each other, so did the Illuminati back both sides during the US Revolution (ref. 13, p. 67).

It has also been reported that Gordonstoun, where Princes' Philip and Charles attended, is, in fact, an elite school set up and controlled by the Illuminati (ref. 13, p. 67).

George Bush senior and junior, and John Major have been offered as leading Freemasons.

Not only was Pike a leading Satanist and member of the Illuminati, but shameful links with this sinister group something that many historians have had difficulty reporting and exposing, for many seem to be unable to say for sure what, if any, his involvement was with the Klan!

KKK members marching off to
perform ghastly ritual!

It is my opinion that Pike had his fingers in many pies, and I believe that he was probably a Darwinist at heart too, for Darwin taught "the white man is superior" to all other races, so Pike would have been very much at home with this Masonic view (Charles Darwin was also a Freemason).

Southerners (Democrats) in the US originally created the Ku Klux Klan after the Civil War.

Author J. Robinson informs us how many of them were Freemasons: "They adopted the circle of the lodge as their formal meeting arrangement for members, named their society for it, and demonstrated their educational level by using the Greek word for "circle," which is kuklos...they styled themselves as the Knights of the Ku Klux Klan...There were hand signals, secret passwords, secret handgrips and recognition signals, even a sacred oath, all adapted from Masonic experience. Some Klansmen even boasted of official connections between the Klan and Freemasonry" (ref. 10, p. 328).

With so much material already in the public domain, I shan't waste time detailing it here. However, I do need to share the following points of fact, which I believe will be of great interest.

The informative DVD Truth Uncovered makes the claim that Pike was indeed a leader of the KKK (ref. 9).

This position is very controversial and difficult to substantiate, but it is my view that Pike was an active member and a leader in the Klan. The reason why this is so difficult to affirm is that many "interested parties" have been able to muddy the waters and put up all types of clever arguments and smoke screens to confuse the researcher, with the hope that they will just give up and return to being ignorant of the actual facts. However, for you the reader, I suggest you take the time and study this further.

At its peak, the KKK was 3 million strong, and

like other infamous and repulsive groups, it was conceived by only a handful of men. In their case, just six. Like their Illuminati friends, this group gave themselves new and secret names like "Grand Magi," "Grand Turk," and "Grand Scribe."

Bradley states that American President Andrew Johnson, who was a Freemason himself, turned a blind eye to these retrogressive steps (new laws being passed against black people), but Congress showed its distaste for the Black Codes by refusing to seat southern Senators in December 1865 (ref. 13, p. 79).

Bill Schnoebelen affirms that Pike was indeed paramount in the organisational structure of this Masonic/racist group: "Pike, on the other hand, helped create what I call 'Masonry in percale,' the Ku Klux Klan! Pike, the old Confederate general, was a wily strategist who knew that if he could leave behind a secret terrorist society in the south to fight against freedom for black people as a rearguard action, the South's defeat might not be in vain. Although these facts may stun Masons, the Lodge has always been racist" (ref. 11, p. 192-193).

Albert Pike once wrote concerning the Klan: "I took my obligation to white men not to Negroes, when I have to accept Negroes as a brother or leave Freemasonry, I will leave it."

Many accept that Pike designed himself the original rituals for the KKK.

THE SKULL AND BONES

When George W. Bush was re-elected in 2004, it was rather ominous to see him place his hand inside a Bible as he took the presidential oath. Most presidents put their hands on the Bible, but rarely inside.

Note the conspicuous hand gesture, far left

Barack Obama would also do the same!

How interesting it was that former US Secretary of State and Roman Catholic John Kerry was not only a fellow Skull and Bones man, but is also George W. Bush's literal blood cousin too.

George W. Bush follows a long line of family members into the sordid Skull and Bones sect, for he was initiated in 1968. His grandfather Prescott Walker was a Nazi sympathiser who not only arranged loans for Hitler but also tried to overthrow the democratically elected Franklin Delano Roosevelt during World War II (ref. 9).

This evil group was created in 1832 by William

Huntington Russell at Yale University (it used to be called "the brotherhood of death").

Russell's family were the US's biggest family of opium smugglers (they made millions shipping opium from Turkey to China) (ref. 9).

IBM Computers designed and helped the Nazis during the Second World War to index millions of imprisoned Jews and others in concentration camps (ref. 9).
IBM also designed tattoos on prisoners' arms. All thanks to the owner, Pa Watson, CEO of IBM (ref. 9).

Ford and General Motors backed Hitler up to the end of the Second World War. No charges of treason were ever brought (ref. 9).

Yet when the CIA in Afghanistan caught the American Taliban soldier, John Walker, he later stood trial in the US and was sentenced to 20 years imprisonment.

"Beware lest any man spoil you through philosophy and vain deceit after the traditions of men, after the rudiments of the world and not after Christ. For in him dwells all the fullness of the Godhead bodily. And ye are complete in him" (Colossians 2:8-9).

McCormick offers the following information: "The originators of Orangeism were Freemasons... Orangeism has also borrowed much in its ritual from Freemasonry" (ref. 2, p. 134). However, Martin Short tells his reader that Martin Smyth, Grand Orange Lodge of Ireland since 1972, was not a freemason on religious grounds: "However, I do not think most Orangemen would share them. Indeed, the fragmentary evidence which I have presented here indicates that the Masonic brotherhood is a substantial behind-the-scenes force in Orange and Unionist politics. Of course, the Craft claims to be non-political but this may simply mean that in Ulster since 1794, its politically-oriented members have simultaneously belonged to Freemasonry's neo-Masonic offshoots: the Orange, Purple and Black" (ref. 15, p. 324).

Short also draws comparisons between the KKK and its Masonic roots to that of other groups: "It seems that wherever Masons have common political aims [the Orange Order, remaining part of the UK], but cannot pursue them through Freemasonry, they set up parallel public movements... only a minority of Orangemen would be socially acceptable in Ulster's Masonic Lodges [because they are working-class, with the Lodge's enjoying middle-class members], but those that are maybe discreetly approached and would probably be pleased to join" (p. 325).

McCormick informs the reader that there are but two degrees in the Orange Order – The Orange and Plain Purple (ref. 2, p. 135).

Members of this sect use passwords, and the word Gideon is what they confess.

For those seeking entrance to the Second Degree (Fellowship Degree), their password is Shibboleth.

In W.P. Malcomson's book, Behind Closed Doors, we get an account of the birth of the Loyal Orange Institution: "The Loyal Orange Institution was formed on 21st September 1795 shortly after the 'Battle of the Diamond' outside Loughall, Co. Armagh. Three well-known local men of this area, James Wilson, Dan Winter, and James Sloan, established the institution. Whilst much is made of these 'founding fathers' within Orange circles; from a spiritual perspective, we see no evidence that any of them had evangelical credentials. History, in fact, shows all three members were dedicated Freemasons and two of the three were actually proprietors of licensed premiers [pubs].....Winter was...an illegal Protestant militia group of the day" (ref. 12, p. 15-16).

July 12 is the main date in the calendar for the lodge, and how unfortunate it was to see some years back, the late Calvinist preacher turned politician Ian Paisley and Orangeman, David Trimble, arm-in-arm during one of their demonstrations again the police, when they enforced a decision to re-route the march.

(Ian Paisley right, David Trimble, left)

Kyle Paisley (behind Paisley in the picture above) one of Ian Paisley's son's, told me via e-mail that his father was not a Freemason, but didn't seem to think anything was wrong with his dad being yoked to the Orange Order. Paisley was, however, a member of the Apprentice Boys of Derry, which has Masonic roots. He also spoke at regular Orange Order meetings.

Malcomson doesn't mince his words when he offers the following: "...the Order is nothing better than veiled Freemasonry embodying much unbiblical error, and therefore worthy of condemnation" (ref. 12, p. 10).

Like their Masonic cousins, there is a secret initiation into this cult, and once again McCormick offers us this sordid account: "The candidate has both trouser legs rolled up above the knees, the left breast is bared and touched with a sharp instrument, he is blindfolded (hoodwinked), led around the Lodge, his bare legs are beaten with a holly-bush or such like-prickly plant; prayers are offered and scripture read. Eventually, he is pushed off a high 'platform' only to be caught in a tarpaulin held by several "brethren." An oath of secrecy is administrated and taken. All this is jocularly referred to as 'The Ride of the Goat'" (ref. 2, p. 137).

It should be pointed out to the reader that the tearing of the shirt and the trouser leg rolled up, dates back to Nimrod: "When, therefore, his suffering was over, and his humiliation past, the clothing in which he was invested was regarded as a meritorious clothing, available not only for himself but for all who were initiated in the mysteries." (A. Hislop, The Two Babylons, p. 183).

Malcomson makes it clear that this "act" is omitted in the Royal Arch Chapter of Ireland (ref. 12, p. 41).

Might I be correct in stating that this type of carrying on, if it were not done voluntarily and in private, would result in people being sectioned under the Mental Health Act of 1952!
(More on this "initiation" later).

What sort of religion is this anyway? Did not the Lord commend the fact that all that He did was in the open, for all to see, and not in secret, just for the "privileged" and "illuminated ones"?

Clearly, Orangeism is a religion much like Masonry is, and Dr M.W. Dewar confirms this in his book Why Orangeism (p. 8).

Legalism seems to dominate this religion, for we are told that the "Worshipful Master's" decision is final and binding, yet does this not clash with the Lord's warning to call no man "master" (Matthew 23:1-12)?

Contrary to reports that the United Protestant Council has rejected the loyal orders having a membership, the fact of the matter is, the lodge has withdrawn from this council, after a membership spanning back some 17 years (The Orange Banner, 2004, Issue 126).

What really put the cat among the pigeons was news that a Baptist church in Lancashire, on 11 September 2004, allowed an Orange wedding to take place. It wasn't the pastor of this church that performed the service, but a reformed vicar who is an Orangeman himself, from another local church.

I should also mention that the sister lodges to Orangeism would be the Royal Arch Purple group, which doesn't enjoy the limelight, and is publicity-shy.

Malcomson has the following to say: "like all Royal Arch Purple men, are oath-bound and never to write down the contents of the degree" (ref. 12, p. 13-14).

This lodge has three degrees:

Orange degree = Entered Apprentice degree (first degree of the Masonic Lodge).

Orange Marksman degree = Fellowship degree (second degree of the Masonic Lodge).

Purple Marksman degree = Master Mason degree (third degree of the Masonic Lodge).

This group also has a shared interest with the pagan druids, for 'they would ascend to the top of some neighbouring hill, and there, towards the close of a summer evening, after the manner of the ancient druids, perform their rites and ceremonies, the meeting being properly styled and guarded' (ref. 12, p. 17).

The following figures, taken from Malcomson's book: "95% of Orangemen today join the Royal Arch Purple Chapter and have therefore been initiated into this degree....anything from up to 95,000 men are subject to the Royal Arch Purple's oath's, rules and teachings...there are only 500,000 Protestant males who live in Northern Ireland, up to one in three Protestants (over the age of 19) could be under the influence of this neo-Masonic structure (including thousands of professing believers)" (ref.

12, p. 23).

Before we leave the Royal Arch Purple Lodge, does any logical and normal person think that a born-again child of God, could agree to the following oath?

"I promise and swear that a Master Mason's secrets...shall remain secure...murder and treason excepted" (ref. 12, p. 29).

One other Ulster group would be the Royal Black Institution.

The late James Molyneaux MP and former member of the Ulster Unionists was the sovereign grandmaster of this group: Cecil Walker (MP for Belfast North) told me how Molyneaux "was a Freemason, having joined in 1966" (ref. 15, p. 324).

It has been reported that Queen Elizabeth II was the grand patroness of world freemasonry (ref. 9).

Masonic looking handshake

Lady initiated into masonry, results in her receiving unbeknown curses, like witchcraft ones

(Incidentally, Windsor is not her family name, but rather Saxe-Coburg-Gotha. The name Windsor was adopted in 1914 to repel anti-German feeling).

Prince Philip was initiated into the Navy Lodge of English Freemasons in London on 5th December 1952 (ref. 2, p. 19). And upon hours of the Duke of Edinburgh's death, The Daily Express, finally affirmed what many of us have long known, that Philip was, in fact, a Master Mason (third-degree). One might have thought he was a thirty-third-degree Mason but for now, anyway, they, the Freemasons are quite comfortable and content reporting him as one of their own!

The same newspaper reported how his son Edward is also a Freemason!

It is claimed by some that the late King George VI and Prince Philip entered Freemasonry by way of the navy as young serving officers, into lodge number 2612. The late Duke of Kent, killed in an air accident in 1942, was also inducted through lodge 2612. His son, the present Duke of Kent, is the grandmaster of the united grand lodge of England.

King George VI proudly dressed
in full Masonic regalia

King Charles, it is claimed, declined Freemasonry membership; nothing is
known of his sons' potential membership into the lodge either. However, at the recent coronation of Charles III, BBC footage of an evening concert seemed to reveal the Masonic compass on the

ground where William was speaking while paying respect to his father.

Masonic-looking handshake between King Charles and Shimon Peres

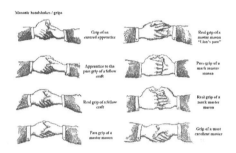

Helpful chart demonstrating Masonic handshakes

When Charles married Camilla, they received a blessing by the archbishop of Canterbury in Windsor Castle; a Masonic chequered pattern was evident for all to see on the floor, especially when they both knelt down to repent of their adultery.

This pattern is also seen in Downing Street, the United Nations, and St. Paul's Cathedral.

The Freemasons were even able to help secure the election of Clement Attlee to the position of leader of the Labour Party in 1935: "According to Hugh Dalton (the future Chancellor of the Exchequer) both Attlee and his rival, Arthur Greenwood, were Masons. Dalton says that a Masonic caucus of MPs and Transport Union officials backed Greenward in the leadership ballot. He came third, so in the run-off, the Masons switched their votes to Brother Attlee" (ref. 15, p. 567).

It is reported Catholic convert Tony Blair is a thirty-third-degree freemason. He is in the same lodge as was Winston Churchill (Studholme Lodge, 1591 and is a Knight of Malta), whilst George W. Bush is a Knight of Enlogia. Both are now Illuminati brothers (ref. 9).

The Palace of Westminster has two Masonic temples. One is called "new welcome Masonic lodge" (ref. 9).

It was also interesting to note how Mr Blair, when only leader of the opposition party in the UK, was invited by Catholic sympathiser and generous donor Rupert Murdock as a guest to his private island off the coast of Australia. Two years later he became one of the UK's youngest prime ministers. Yet, when John Smith died, Tony Blair had not been the favourite to replace him.

The same can be said when Jimmy Carter was standing for US president. Only 4% of Democrats supported him, yet the following quote from US Senator Barry Goldwater shines some interesting light on how politics and secret societies go hand-in-hand: "They mobilized the money power of the Wall Street bankers, the intellectual influence of the academic community – which is subservient to the wealth of the great tax-free foundations – and the media controllers represented in the membership of the CFR, and the Trilateral" (ref. 13, p. 139).

And why did they pull out all of the stops for him? Because David Rockefeller knew they could do "business" with this millionaire professing Christian peanut farmer from Georgia.

1/6 of police officers in the UK are practising freemasons (ref. 9).

The British police force (now called "police service") has a chequered black and white pattern around their cap badges.

(The freemasons introduced this in the late 1970s. Every lodge in the world has a black and white pattern on its floors. Also outside New Scotland Yard, there is a revolving pyramid. Again this is Masonic).

There are around 600,000 freemasons in the UK (ref. 9).

The UK has 8,600 lodges (ref. 5).

There are 700 lodges in the whole of Ireland, with 560 of them in the north, and 143 in the south (ref. 15, p. 325).

The US government has 666 members in their constitution. Coincidence or something more sinister – you decide?

President Gerard Ford shamelessly
displays his Shriner hat

The American founders were all practising freemasons (6), and if one looks on the back of their money, you will see the eye of Horus, better known as Satan. Most Americans have no idea of this (ref. 12, p.109).

J.R. Church, from his book, Guardians of the Grail, makes the following prognosis: "The symbol may represent a god, but it is not the God of the Bible. It is a human eye indicating that man is god" (p. 165).

I remember when I went to the Washington mint before I was saved, and during one of the daily walkabouts, I asked the guide what the single eye meant. And she replied, "I don't know sir. I think it might be God's"? Sorry, but the God of the Bible does not have only one eye!

There is also a Latin inscription underneath the pyramid – *mottos e Pluribus Unum* – (out of many one) and *Novus Ordo Seclorum* (a new order of the ages, or "the new world order" – "a secular state," my words and emphasis) (ref. 4, p. 5).

Berry also offers the following on other symbols on the dollar bill: "...the all seeing eye, the number of feathers on the eagle's spread wings, the stars above the eagle's head in the shape of the Star of David" (ref. 4, p. 5).

What Berry omits to mention, however, is that the eagle is, in fact, a phoenix, and these symbols were introduced in 1933, by thirty-third-degree Freemason Franklin D. Roosevelt (the same year he introduced emergency powers to be given to him).

The Lord Jesus Christ was 33 years old when He died for the sins of the world. The Freemasons, under the inspiration of the devil, connivingly counterfeit this with their 33-level structure.

For example, thirty-three stones make up the pyramid. There are thirty-three levels in Freemasonry. Pope John Paul I was 33 days into his papacy when he was sacrificed/"died." Coincidence or not, you decide?

This is an Illuminati plan to control America, create a federal Europe and then have a single world government (13 p. 64), regardless of who the incumbent US president is, for all US presidents have been Freemasons (ref. 6).

Hollywood actor, Glenn Ford, thirty-second-degree freemason

In Michael Bradley's book The Secret Societies Handbook, he notes the following:"…A close examination of a map of Washington, D.C., reveals that they [US Founders] hid their two most important occult symbols, the pentagram (five-pointed star) and the "Square and Compass" at the heart of the United States" (p. 51-52).
(More on this later)

Former Freemason Charles Finney lines up with his pound of flesh when he offers the following about how the Freemasons controlled most of the US in his day… "Nearly all the civil offices in the country were in the hands of Freemasons; and that the press was completely under their control, and almost altogether in their hands...I do not recollect a magistrate, or a constable, or sheriff in that country that was not at that time a Freemason" (ref. 15, p. 5).

Please see how the US political and constitutional breakdown goes:

(1) President
(14) Cabinet Members
(100) Senators
(435) Representatives
(9) Supreme Court Justices
(13) Appeal Court Justices
(90) District Court Chief Justices
(4) Territory Justices
= 666

First-degree Freemason Nathan Bedford
Forrest's suspicious hand gesture

When using Latin numerals, Washington and New York, both equal, 666.
Hitler was into esoteric levels of Freemasonry. He

sought to wipe out the main sections and lodges and turn them into a full occult system (ref. 6).

The Alamo is dedicated to the Freemasons (ref. 6).

There are approximately 4 million freemasons in America (ref. 4, p. 4).

Washington, D.C., is designed in a pentagram, with the Goat of Mendes' head at the centre.

The Washington Monument is dedicated to Freemason George Washington.

The Pentagon is designed with a five-point pentagram.

The Statue of Liberty was donated by French Freemasons to American Freemasons (ref. 6).

Congregational medals of honour are pentagrams, designed by Freemasons (ref. 6).

The Nazi Iron Cross was a Masonic symbol (ref. 14).

The seal of the U.S. is Masonic (ref. 6).

The presidential seal is Masonic (ref. 6).

The Star of David is carefully coded on the U.S. one-dollar bill (ref. 14).

The grand lodge of Israel incorporates the Star of David into their Masonic symbol, with the capital "G" in the centre (ref. 14).

World War II was a Masonic plan (ref. 6).

The Catholic Mafia was founded by a Sicilian Masonic terrorist organisation (ref. 11, p. 192).

Writer Schnoebelen states the mafia and the Illuminati share certain rituals (ref. 11, p. 192).

Married men, upon entering the blue lodge, are told to remove their wedding rings during their inauguration into Freemasonry.

The Blue Lodge has three levels:

Apprentice
Fellow Craft
Master Mason

They also hold to the following beliefs:

The Fatherhood of God
The Brotherhood of Man
The Immorality of the Soul

Not only does the potential Freemason have to study the ritual, which can be very long and tedious, but he/she also has to pay for each degree they enter into.

Once again, this religion is not for ordinary poor people, but for those with disposable cash. Schnoebelen tells us that the first degree would cost you $50. The second is $100, with the third degree costing $150 (ref. 11, p. 54).

Schnoebelen also offers the following about those who wish to be fast-tracked: "If the new Master Mason is perceived to be a Christian, quite often he will be directed to the York Rite since that has

"Christian degrees." If the Mason is more secular, or perhaps in a bit of a hurry, he is advised to go the route of Scottish Rite, which rockets you through twenty-nine degrees in a couple of weekends, and enables you to go on and join the Shrine" (ref. 11, p. 55).

The York rite has ten degrees.

The Scottish rite has thirty-two degrees (thirty-third is honorary, which Ronald Regan received when still at the White House, on 11th February 1988) (ref. 10, p. 325).

Most will never go past the last degree – even Joseph Smith of the Mormons never went higher than the third degree, although he was expelled from the lodge for stealing their secrets. Brigham Young, however, made the thirty-second degree.

It should be noted that women, although restricted from witnessing their husband's inauguration, have their own form of Freemasonry, through the Eastern Star wing "Rainbow Girls," and "Job's Daughters" exists for young ladies (ref. 4, p. 4).

Glamorous looking ladies happily
pictured in their Masonic apparel

John Robinson also tells us that only 1% of black males are Freemasons (ref. 10, p. 329). Their lodge is called "Prince Hall Masonry" with Jessie Jackson, Nat King Cole, and Colin Powell representing them.

No doubt Barack Obama and Nelson Mandela would have been initiated into the lodge too.

One shouldn't be surprised, however, to note how the lodge seems only interested in middle or upper-class clientele.

The word 'free' mason simply means to be freeborn, i.e., never having been a slave (ref. 4, p. 8-9).

"Christian" Freemasons are never allowed to end a prayer in the name of Jesus, during services.

While blindfolded and with a noose around his neck, he kneels at an altar, with his hands tied.

Blood oaths are then taken from the new applicant. While taking these mandatory oaths, the applicant is now affirming that should he reveal lodge secrets, then the following consequences will occur to him:

(a) His throat will be cut from ear to ear; his tongue ripped out
(b) Chest ripped open; heart ripped out
(c) Belly ripped open and his bowels and intestines will spill on the ground

Upon the initiation, the freemason (first degree) will be expected to make the following obligation: "....I most solemnly and sincerely promise and swear, that I will always hail, ever conceal, and never reveal, any of the arts, parts or points of the hidden mysteries of ancient Freemasonry....under no less a penalty than that of having my throat cut across, my tongue torn out by its roots, and buried in the rough sand of the sea at low water mark where the tide ebbs and flows twice in twenty-four hours, should I ever knowingly or willingly violate my solemn oath and obligation as an Apprentice Mason. So help me, God" (ref. 13, p. 55).

We all know of doggy Masonic handshakes, but Freemasons have other methods of identifying one another, with questions like, "What is the time?" Or, "How old are you?" If you answer 9:30 or 50 years, this shows you are not a "brother."
The correct answer is, "There is no time any longer" or "I am very old." And when a Mason 'brother' needs to be identified by another 'brother,' he will say, "I'm on the level."

Their members, to symbolise 'divine purity' and a shield of protection for them when they stand before the Great White Throne Judgment, wear white aprons.

Freemasons have no real concept of sin or salvation within the lodge. Much like the cults, the emphasis is on works and good living, and improvements to one's life are sufficient to be saved, i.e., good works and lots of good deeds should guarantee entrance to "Mason heaven" (ref. 7, p. 13).

Former high-level Freemason, Jim Shaw, offers us the following: "Faith in the atonement of Jesus has nothing to do with it; it is rather a matter of enlightenment, step by step, which comes with initiation into the Masonic degrees and their mysteries" (ref. 4, p. 33).

Ankerberg quotes the following source Masonic Ritual and Monitor about the Celestial Lodge Above: "He who wears the lambskin as a badge of a Mason is thereby continually reminded of purity of life and conduct which is essentially necessary to his gaining admission into that celestial Lodge above, where the Supreme Architect of the Universe presides" (ref. 7, p. 14).

Demonic names such as Abaddon (Revelation 9:11) are recited in lodges.

Only 2% of what the Shriners raise for charity goes to good works. The rest goes to themselves (ref. 11, p. 208).
(Shriners wear a red hat, which represent Christian martyrs that were killed for their faith in Christ, in 700 AD).

Only a thirty-second-degree Scottish-rite Freemason is permitted to be a Shriner (ref. 4, p. 5).

Worldwide, there are 100,000 lodges (ref. 13, p. 52).

The Freemasons orchestrated the Russian and French Revolutions, for most of the revolutionists were Freemasons. This period was known as "the great terror" (5).

Jack the Ripper used many Masonic methods when carving up his victims. In his 1977 book, Jack the Ripper – The Final Solution, the author Stephen Knight compares some Masonic coincidences concerning the unfortunate women who were victims of the ripper. 1) Throat cutting of the five women was from left to right. 2) A five-star pentagram, both in the body location, and markings on the face of Kate Eddows. 3) Mitre Square in London, where one of the murders was committed, is located in the secretive city of London with its own Masonic surroundings. Sadly Knight died aged 33 (another coincidence or something more sinister?)

Yet his brilliant and ingenious book highlights perhaps more of the mysterious acts of Freemasons, rather than the true identity of the Ripper.

New Freemasons blasphemously chant, "I am what I am." This is one of the Biblical and sacred names of the God of the Bible. The one and only true God (Exodus 3:14; John 8:28).

Their "holy communion" is similar to that of Catholicisms communion of the dead.

They mock the death and resurrection of the Lord

Jesus Christ by focusing their attention on a dubious fable concerning King Hiram, whom they believe (even though there is absolutely no proof of this) died and was miraculously raised from the dead.

Shaw comments on this: "It is the consensus of opinion among the Masonic authorities, philosophers and writers of doctrine that the legend of Hiram Abiff is merely the Masonic version of a much older legend, that of Isis and Osiris, basis of the Egyptian Mysteries" (ref. 4, p. 28).

All American presidents have been Freemasons (ref. 6), except Roman Catholic Jack Kennedy, who may have been the Catholic equivalent, a Knight of Columbus with membership in the U.S. is 1.3 million, and possibly Joe Biden too (ref. 10, p. 330).

It is not clear whether or not Donald Trump is a Freemason. He attended the church of the Freemason Norman Vincent Peale for many years, so it would be logical to think Peale would have at least approached Trump in the early days of his property enterprise to join the lodge.

Here is a list of notable members:

Benjamin Franklin and Thomas Jefferson (who was also a Rosicrucian 13 p. 123) and members of the Illuminati, along with Joseph Stalin (ref. 5).

Edger Hoover and L.B.J. were both members of the Washington Lodge.

Israeli Prime Ministers Yitzhak Rabin, Shimon Peres, and Benjamin Netanyahu are/were Freemasons. Rabin joined in the 1960s and led a major convention in Jerusalem in 1976 (ref. 14).

It is reported that Netanyahu was recruited when Ambassador to the UN in the 1980s.
The Jerusalem Post (11/94) affirmed that Rabin and Peres were Freemasons, when they ran an advert,

from 'The Grand Lodge of the State of Israel,' to the Masons of Peace.

The late King Hussein of Jordan was a Freemason, as is his son (ref. 14).

Former president Hosni Mubarak of Egypt was also a Freemason (ref. 14).

Vladimir Lenin and Leon Trotsky were thirty-first-degree Freemasons.

All five founders of the USSR were Freemasons (ref. 14).

Winston Churchill, after World War II, spoke of a "new world order," and a "United States of Europe." He was savaged and attacked in the press and parliament for this, but he was, nonetheless, 70 years ahead of his time.

Salvador Allende.

Lord Horatio Nelson.

Christopher Wren (architect of St. Paul's Cathedral).

Paul Revere.

Duke Ellington.

Count Basie.

John Wayne (later converted to Catholicism on his deathbed, as did Nat King Cole).

It is believed that Wolfgang Amadeus Mozart was murdered for revealing Masonic secrets in his opera The Magic Flute (ref. 10, p. 177).

VATICAN CONNECTION

It has been widely accepted that the Vatican banker Roberto Calvi was murdered by Freemasons in London, on 18 June 1982, under Blackfriars Bridge. With bricks stuffed into his suit pockets, interestingly he had shaved off his trademark moustache that he had grown since a young man just before he was murdered. Many suspect he was hounded by the Vatican to his cruel terrible fate, to die cold and alone under a deserted and desolate bridge.

Calvi's grieving family still pursues this matter through the courts to clear his name.

McCormick has the following to say about the hypocrisy of the Catholic church: "If Vatican involvement with P2 and Banco Ambrosiano was so deep that its money was being used to supply Argentina with the means to buy missiles to fight the Falklands War, while the Pope visited Britain and Argentina, then it was decided that to avoid further damaging exposures, the Masons must be protected and embraced" (ref. 2, p. 104).

Mormon Freemason, J.D. Lee, was ordered by Brigham Young to murder hundreds of Bible-believing Christians: "I knew of many men being killed in Nauvoo by the Danites. It was the rule that all the enemies of Joseph Smith should be killed, and I know of many a man who was quietly put out of the way by the orders of Joseph Smith and his apostles while the church was there..." (Confessions, 1880 ed., p. 284).

Former Freemason and former Mormon Ed Decker had to flee from a speaking engagement in Scotland after the Freemasons had poisoned him. His own father (a Freemason too) renounced him for many years, only to be reconciled on his deathbed. Decker was able to get his father to repent of his masonry and receive Jesus Christ as his own Lord and Saviour. He died a happy and saved man.

Finney would also record how the following murder was orchestrated and carried out by the Freemasons because of one William Morgan, an individual who had exposed the lodge through his explosive writings. He quotes one of the assailants who later confessed to his involvement in this murder: "Henry L. Valance, who acknowledged himself to have been one of the three who was selected to make a final disposition of the ill-fated victim of Masonic vengeance... Morgan, on being informed of their proceedings against him, demanded by what authority they had condemned him, and who were his judges. 'He commenced wringing his hands and talking of his wife and children, the recollections of whom, in that awful hour, terribly affected him. His wife, he said, was young and inexperienced, and his children were but infants....they gave him one-half hour to prepare for his 'inevitable fate.'

Finney's account concluded with this man, with

weights secured firmly to his body, then being thrown alive into the river and left to drown. "They also kidnapped Mr Miller, the publisher, but the citizens of Batavia, finding it out, pursued the kidnappers, and finally rescued him."

It is also noted in this book how the publicity of this case was so devastating to the Masons, that "two thousand lodges were suspended. The ex-president of a western college, who is himself a Freemason, has recently published some very important information on the subject, though he justifies Masonry. He says that, out of a little more than fifty thousand Masons in the United States at that time, forty-five thousand turned their backs upon the lodge to enter the lodge no more" (ref. 15, p. 7-8).

Charles Finney: "Without consulting anyone, I finally went to the Lodge and requested my discharge. My mind was made up. Withdraw from them I must – with their consent if I might; without this consent, if I must. Of this I said nothing, but somehow it came to be known that I had withdrawn...I found that in taking these oaths I had been grossly deceived and imposed upon. I had been led to suppose that there were some very important secrets to be communicated to me, but in this, I found myself entirely disappointed. Indeed I came to the deliberate conclusion that my oaths had been procured by fraud and misrepresentations; that the institution was in no respect what I had been informed it was; and as I have had the means of examining it more thoroughly, it has become more and more irresistibly plain to me that Masonry is highly dangerous to the State, and in every way injurious to the Church of Christ...Judging from unquestionable evidence, how can we fail to pronounce Freemasonry an unchristian institution? We can see that its morality is unchristian. Its oath-bound secrecy is unchristian. The administration and taking of its oaths are unchristian and a violation of the positive command of Christ..."

W.S. Jacoby: "Until I converted to Christ I was a notoriously wicked man and dissipated...I spent a small fortune in years of dissipation while a member of my lodge, and yet no minister in the lodge ever exhorted me to desist from my reckless course or offered to direct me to the Lamb of God, who takes away the sins of the world."

This last quote reminds me of a gentleman, who was an elder in the Brethren Assembly and was also the leader of my local council. Yet I once asked his old colleague, the former mayor, whether or not he had ever witnessed to him, the answer came back, no!

He knew this councillor was a professing Christian, but like so many people, his religion was a private one, much like mine was in the church of Rome before I was saved out of it, something Scripture condemns (Ezekiel 3:18-21; Acts 20:26).

Shaw: "Masonry, contrary to popular belief, is not based on the Bible. Masonry is actually based on the Kabala, a medieval book of magic and mysticism" (ref. 4, p. 18).

Herman Newmark: "One condition of Freemasonry... you must believe in God; but who or what is meant by "God" *does not matter at all.* Suppose my god is the sun, and my fellow mason's god is the moon, and someone else worships a block of stone or his ancestors...*then he is a fit person for the Masonic lodge*, for all races and religions and creeds may meet here to worship their own god....so long as they agree on one common *word* "God" (*Why I Am Not a Mason*, p. 2).

THE DANGEROUS STRUCTURE OF FREEMASONRY

The Duke of Kent leads a celebration for the
275th anniversary of the Grand Lodge

Worldwide Freemasonry can be viewed as two sets
of ascending stairs that begin and end together. Any
eager young man that takes his first hesitant steps
into the unknown world of Freemasonry starts his
journey with the first three steps.

They are:

1st Degree: Entered Apprentice
2nd Degree: Fellow craft
3rd Degree: Master Mason
Most men will be content to rest in this popular
position because by now they will have learnt the
secret handshakes and other rituals peculiar to this
rite.

The first three degrees now form the Blue Lodge of
Masonry.

Later they will also have to decide at this point of time whether to either accept the Scottish Rite or the York Rite.

SCOTTISH RITE

The popular Scottish Rite is represented with 30 steps or degrees. Personal mystic names will be granted to him in his journey to reach the highest pinnacle in Masonry.

Five known Masonic figures of the past will meet and accompany him, and it is stated, guide him in his journey. These are King Solomon, King Cyrus, Sultan, Acolyte and George Washington.

Each degree is supposed to teach a moral. To earn a new degree the candidate must prepare himself for what will be asked and expected of him as he examines and learns the rituals.

The thirty-second degree is the highest degree a participating mason can ever hope to achieve.

The acclaimed thirty-third degree will be awarded to him, if he gets there, by members of the shadowy Supreme Council governing body of the Rite.

The Scottish Rite was started by exiled Scottish migrants in France. If, and he does have a choice, he might decide to journey through the York Rite.

YORK RITE

The York Rite, according to legend, derives its name from York in England. It was the first Masonic body to be organised. The journeying mason in the York Rite advances thorough ten degrees. These are known by a name and not by a number.

They are as following:

Master Mark
Past Master (Virtual)
Most Excellent Master
Royal Arch Mason
Royal Master
Select Master
Super Excellent Master
Order of the Red Cross
Order of the Knights of Malta
Order of the Knights Temple

FURTHER SCOTTISH RITE DEGREES

4th Secret Master
5th Perfect Master
6th Intimate Secretary
7th Provost and Judge
8th Intendant of the Building
9th Master elect of nine elu of the nine
10th Elect of fifteen elu of the fifteen
11th Sublime master elected elu of the twelve
12th Grand Master Architect: Master Architect
13th Master of the Ninth Arch: Royal Arch of Solomon
14th Grand Elect Mason
15th Knight of the East or Sword
16th Prince of Jerusalem
17th Knight of the East and West
18th Knight of the Rose Cross
19th Grand Pontiff
20th Master Ad Vitam: Master of the Symbolic Lodge
21st Patriarch Noachite
22nd Prince of Libanus: Knight of the Royal Arch
23rd Chief of the tabernacle
24th Prince of the tabernacle
25th Knight of the Brazen Serpent
26th Prince of mercy
27th Commander of the temple
28th Knight of the Sun
29th Knight of St. Andrew
30th Grand Elect Knight

31st Grand Inspector Inquisitor
32nd Sublime Prince of the Royal Secret
33rd Sovereign Grand Inspector

There is continual confusion whether or not Freemasonry is actually a religion?

According to one authority on the subject, Joseph Newton, an Episcopal minister: "Masonry is not a religion, but is religious." He further qualifies this by stating: "It is not a church but a worship, in which men of all religions may unite."

The problem with this aspect of masonry is that it hints of monism, which is derived from the Greek word for one. This has its many tangled roots in Hinduism, which today permeates many religions that openly worship many gods. All of them are false.

Freemasonry would openly suggest that Christianity is but one religion among many others. No lodge could or would, wish to bring offence to its members who practise other assorted religions. Sadly the Bible is adjusted to fit the beliefs of Freemasonry with any references to Jesus Christ, either played down or omitted. In I Peter 2:5, the last three words: by Jesus Christ are deliberately left out or passed over. No prayers, we are informed, are ever offered in the lodges, in the name of Jesus Christ.

In John 8:12, we are graphically informed by Jesus, that He is the light of the world. Those who do not follow Him, walk in darkness.

This must I suggest be a clear warning to Freemasons to get out of this false system. And quickly!

In Matthew 6:24, the Lord says: "No man can serve two masters."

This promotes for the mason an ongoing conflict between Freemasonry and Christianity.

To resolve this problem for the mason he must do three things immediately:

1) Get out of masonry and all of its other contagious habits. 2) Get out of all organised religions. They remain deeply flawed and incapable of salvation. 3) He must be saved.

To do this, the apostle Paul tells us: "If thou shalt confess with thy mouth that Jesus is Lord, and shalt believe in thine heart that God has raised Him from the dead, thou shalt be saved" (Romans 10:9).

As far as I know, the Illuminati has twelve degrees, each represented by a personal name.

MASONIC STREETS IN WASHINGTON

A MAP OF WASHINGTON D.C. SHOWING MASONIC
SYMBOLS BUILT INTO STREETS

"When the Freemasons and occultists designed Washington D.C., they incorporated their Masonic symbols into the streets of the city...I showed this map to a leading Mason, who replied: 'It must have happened by accident.' Of interest is the fact that the goat's horns fit into the two top areas of the pentagram, his face in the middle, his ears to the sides but please note where the beard stops-right at the White House, so ultimately, let's face it, the President of the U.S.A. is spiritually affected from at least two areas of the occult world. Therefore, is it not reasonable to assume that the city of Washington D.C. is under a terrible Luciferian curse" (Barry R. Smith, Better Than Nostradamus, 1996, p. 68-71).

Whatever happened to separation of Church and

State?

How would you honestly feel if this were your son, brother, father or husband, during their secret initiation into the Masonic lodge?

One thing is quite certain: there is no absolute truth outside of the Holy Bible. As far as I am concerned, this material is quite plausible and perhaps even probable. But I would certainly encourage you the reader to do further research.

The patriarch of the Rothschild banking family once said: "Give me control over a nation's economy, and I care not who writes the laws."

God would also say: "The love of money is the root of all evil?"

So who's side are you rooting for now?

I would also like to add, that those in the conspiracy community are divided on certain aspects of the New World Order, so common sense and an open mind is needed to decipher the following information.

They created the theory of evolution, atheism, communism, anarchism and socialism; and they mock people who have bought into it by making a living from it.

An interesting and very rare quote from the Catholic church: "We [the Illuminati] have spread the spirit of revolt and false liberalism among the nations of the Gentiles so as to persuade them away from their faith and even make them ashamed of professing the precepts of their Religion and obeying the Commandments of their Church. We have brought many of them to boast of being atheists, and more than that, to glory in being descendants of the ape! We have given them new theories, impossible of realisation, such as Communism, Anarchism, and Socialism, which are now serving our purpose... The stupid Gentiles have accepted them with the greatest enthusiasm, without realising that those theories are ours and that they constitute our most powerful instruments against themselves" (The Catholic Gazette, February 1936).

Of £16 million received for Masonic charities only

£1.35 million, that's just 8%, went to Masonic charities.

King Edward VIII, the Duke of Windsor, King George VI and Prince Michael of Kent, were each thirty-three degree Masons. The historian, and former Freemason, Andrew Roberts correctly remarked, that when King Edward VIII abdicated, he used a Masonic handshake to say goodbye to his brother, George.

The following extracts are taken from Masonic literature: "So then, because our ancient brethren-'the old sun-worshippers'-met on the highest hills to worship Baal or the sun-god, and freemasonry being that same worship revived, it must necessarily follow, that Masonic lodges must be held in the highest rooms of buildings, to carry out the coincidence" (*The Master's Carpet*, Edmond Ronayne, p. 247.) "Masonry has nothing whatsoever to do with the bible, that it is not founded on the bible, for if it were it would not be masonry, it would be something else" (*Digest of Masonic Law*, p. 207-209.)

"Whether you swear or take God's name in vain, don't matter so much. Of course, the name Lord Jesus Christ, as you know, don't amount to anything, but Mah-hah-bone – o, horror! You must never, on any account, speak that awful name aloud. That would be a most heinous crime....un-masonic - unpardonable" (The Masonic Handbook, p.184.)

"When a brother reveals any of our great secrets; whenever, for instance, he tells anything about Boaz, or Tubalcain, or Jachin or that awful Mah-hah-bone, or even whenever a minister prays in the name of Christ in any of our assemblies, you must always hold yourself in readiness, if called upon, to cut his throat from ear to ear, pull out his tongue by the roots and bury his body at the bottom of some lake or pond" (The Masonic Handbook, p. 74.)

The Illuminati succeeded in destroying nations patriotism, currency and faith.
Groups that were used to do this were Hollywood, feminism, civil rights movement, governments and others.

Films and radio broadcasts contain subliminal messages.

The American Civil Liberty Union not only had the Bible removed from schools, but they are also credited for assisting the American Nazi Party and spoke out for a teacher, who wanted to teach evolution (Encyclopaedia Americana, Grolier International, Inc., 1980, p. 680-681.)

Members of the Illuminati often meet in Masonic Lodges.

The United Nations is the Illuminati's Head Office. And it cost John D. Rockefeller $18 million as a "gift" to the UN to purchase this 18-acre real estate (The World Book Encyclopaedia, Vol. 20, p. 24.)

As Sinn Fein is the political wing for the IRA, so the Council on Foreign Relations (CFR) is the political mouthpiece for the Illuminati.

President George Washington wrote the following about his satisfaction of the Illuminati: "It is not my intention to doubt that the doctrine of the Illuminati and the principles of Jacobinism had not spread to the United States. On the contrary, no one is more satisfied of this fact than I am" (Fourth Reich of the Rich, Griffin.)

They masterminded the US Civil War for the purpose of putting America into debt, with the purpose of creating the National Bank.

European and British bankers financed Trotsky, Lenin and Stalin, before, during and after the Russian Revolution. (Lenin used to be known as Vladimir Ilyich Ulyanov).

"After being thrown out of France and Spain, Leon Trotsky and his family arrived in New York aboard the streamer Monserrat on January 13, 1917. Although he was never known to have a job, the Trotsky's lived in a fashionable apartment and travelled around in a chauffeured limousine. Trotsky left New York aboard the S.S. Kristianiafjord bound for Petrograd to organize the Bolshevik phase of the Russian Revolution. When the ship docked at Halifax, Nova Scotia, on April 3, 1917, the Trotsky party was detained by Canadian authorities under instructions received by the British Admiralty in London. Within hours, great pressure was brought to bear on Canadian authorities by high officials in both Washington and London to [release them]... recently declassified by the Canadian government, reveal that the authorities knew that Trotsky's group were 'Socialists' leaving (American) for the purpose of starting [a] revolution against the present Russian government. History must never forget that Woodrow Wilson, despite the efforts of the British police, made it possible for Leon Trotsky to enter Russia with an American passport" (Wall Street and the Bolshevik, Anthony G. Sutton, pgs. 25-28.)

Communism and Socialism were pretty much the same and were only able to succeed, due to 'outside help,' from London, Paris and New York.

Franklin D. Roosevelt gave Eastern Europe to the communists after the Second World War.

Jacob Schiff gave $20 million in gold to help the final triumph of Bolshevism in Russia (William Josiah Sutton, The Illuminati 666, p. 239.)

Karl Marx was a correspondence and political analyst for Horace Greeley, owner of the New York Times. In 1849 both Horace Greeley and Clinton Roosevelt financially assisted the Communist league in London, in the publication of the Communist Manifesto. There are two cheques (checks) made payable to Marx by Nathan

Rothschild, which can be seen on display at the British Museum in London (William Josiah Sutton, The Illuminati 666, pg. 201.)

Human sacrifices and the consumption of their blood is something the elite and their cohorts are known to participate in. Celebrities and VIPS also are reported to indulge in this wicked act (Jeremiah 32:35).

JFK, like Tony Blair, made his pilgrim trip to the pyramids to worship the 'gods.'

The pope of Freemasonry, Albert Pike and leader of the Illuminati in the US, announced that three world wars would be needed to implement the new world order. Albert Pike also belonged to a Luciferian group known as Palladist: "The latter group, with which we are mainly concerned, was known under the alternative names of Luciferians and Palladists. They were said to adore Lucifer, the equal of Adonai, Jahweh. He was in their view 'the God of Light,' the good principle, while Adonai was 'the God of darkness,' the evil principle.

In short, he was Satan himself. This worship was founded on a dualistic philosophy and was a sort of topsy-turvy Christianity.

The name of Palladist is derived from a palladium which they were said to revere, namely the Baphomet, or grotesque idol, the worship of which was one of the articles of accusations against the

"Knights Templars" in the fourteenth century.

It was alleged that the Baphomet was preserved in secret through nearly five centuries after the suppression of the order and ultimately carried by one Isaac Long in 1801, together with the skull of the last Grand Master, the unhappy Jacques du Molay, from Paris to Charleston in the United States of America.

These relics were averred to have there become the sacred objects of a society, which was a development of Freemasonry. The head of the society, we are told, was one Albert Pike, under whose influence it spread all over the civilised world" (Encyclopaedia of Religion and Ethics, Vol. 12, p. 204.)

An Anglican Masonic Chaplain

This is one of those frequently asked questions that regularly gets an airing either on Christian radio or in church circles. Another question asked: "Is freemasonry Christian?" I must answer an emphatic no to both questions, and also ponder the wider question, why would any Bible believing Christian seek membership into the Freemasons or any secret society for that matter?

The former archbishop of Canterbury, Geoffrey Fisher was a practising Freemason all his life, and he wasn't the only one!

The Church of England has long had the problem of how to deal with Freemasons in their 'broad church.' The former archbishop of Canterbury, Rowan Williams, whose father was in the lodge, used to block the promotion of practising Masonic bishops before he was promoted to Canterbury.

(Whilst Williams never confessed to being a mason himself, he is a proud member of the druids, a group that historically sacrificed children to appease their gods).

This is the infamous Masonic chequered floor, which can be seen on British police force uniforms, and inside Number 10 Downing Street, not to mention in numerous other government institutions

Other well known "Christian" Freemasons have been Charles Taze Russell of the Jehovah's Witnesses, and the husband of Ellen White of the Seventh Day Adventists.

In Martin Short's acclaimed book Inside the Brotherhood, he shares the following account of one Anglican Primate who wasn't happy to learn of a Masonic burial in an Anglican church: "I found that the words 'Jesus Christ' were omitted from the prayers and the word 'Architect' substituted. Worse still, the cross was to be removed from the altar...I thought that in this case, it would be better for the service to take place in a Masonic temple....this line I took stirred up a hornets' nest. I was warned that I had offended important benefactors and that the diocese would suffer financially. It might have done so" (p. 76- 77).

In recent years the Freemasons have tried hard to reinvent their shady and suspicious image, by allowing members of the press and public to come and visit their lodges, but certainly not whilst their ghastly rituals are in operation.

One recent Masonic newsletter that was sent to me, had the following quote, about the need for more 'good news stories' to be made known to the local press: "...Now that we are achieving good coverage in the local press we are looking to other means of spreading the good news about freemasonry."

The same publication boasted of the numerous good works that they do in their local areas, with the sum raised for charity, for the year 2004/2005, being £200,037.

It sadly appears that they are trusting in their own good works to save them from their sins and not in Jesus Christ's finished work on the cross (Romans 10:1-4.)

I must state categorically that to the best of my knowledge there have never been any practising Freemasons in my immediate family. How could there be? As a Catholic family before my salvation, had not Rome forbidden membership to Freemasonry? At least officially and in the open they had, and by no less than nine papal bulls, issued by fuming popes!

All this was to change covertly and successfully, however, after Vatican II, when I suspect the ecumenical plot allowed the Freemasons to join the fold. Or maybe the Freemasons had always been in the Curia. One should remember the notorious Vatican P2 lodge, which consisted of many high-ranking cardinals and politicians. But if you're still not sure of the Catholic view on this, just check their 1994 catechism, where you'll find no mention of Freemasonry and why a Catholic cannot seek membership of this anti-Christ movement.

Today I don't think they – the hierarchy – could care less what you wish to do with your spare time. Except promote the social gospel and seek a greater 'unity' amongst the world's religions. Certainly, they wouldn't encourage a thorough Bible study or examine how sinners are actually saved by trusting in the precious blood of Christ alone, not by one's good works and useless rituals.

So back to my main question of should a Christian be a Freemason? I must answer my own question with a question: why would he want to (and yes, I know some lodges allow women as has been stated already), as the Order of the Eastern Star, but they remain very much male driven.

Incidentally, the Knights of DeMolay are a related organisation that a young Bill Clinton was attracted to join when he was just 15-years-old.

(It is pretty much known how the world's economic, political, and entertainment leaders are either Protestant Freemasons or Catholic Knights of Malta or Columbus.

According to Freemasonry Today, young Bill enlisted in DeMolay at Hot Springs in Arkansas in 1961. He later stated: "I enjoyed learning all parts of the ritual. I grew up in a family with no money and no political influence. I had a lot of breaks; a lot of people helped me. DeMolay I think helps that."

He would later become a Rhodes scholar. Cecil Rhodes was himself a highly respected millionaire, Freemason.

The writer George L. Hunt states that: "Secretism is not only non-Christian but that it is anti-Christian."

Heavy stuff you may say but are they religious, these Freemasons? They most certainly are! Just listen to what Albert Pike, 'Sovereign Pontiff' (sounds very popish') of universal Freemasonry had to say: "Every Masonic lodge is a temple of religion."

Or Albert Mackey, who wrote The Encyclopaedia of Freemasonry: "Masonry is an eminently religious institution. The truth is masonry is undoubtedly a religious institution."

And what about a British Knight of the Realm, Sir John Cockburn, past deputy 'Grand Master' of South Australia, who said: "Masonry is a form of worship in which all religions can unite." (And, boy, aren't they just promoting that today?)

According to the author Jim Shaw, himself a previous thirty-third degree Freemason, who was wonderfully saved out of the darkness of Freemasonry and brought into the glorious light of Jesus Christ, he offered the following:

"Masonry, contrary to popular belief, is not based upon the Bible. Masonry is actually based on the Kabala, a medieval book of magic and mysticism."

This accurate statement is also reinforced by no less than Albert Pike. He said: "Masonry is a search after light. That search leads us directly back, as you see, to the Kabala."

Now if there is one thing that I have always been clear about is that people must get out of organised religion! Have nothing to do with it. It cannot save you! No two ways about it!

I mean why would you wish to be mixed up with these people anyway. And one should also be mindful to the fact that Freemasonry excludes the name of the Lord Jesus from prayer, and His exclusiveness for salvation.

The precious name of Jesus is excluded from every passage of Scripture that is read in the lodge.

For example, this verse is how it should read, but Freemasons omit the following underlined words: "Now we command you, brethren, <u>in the name of our Lord Jesus Christ</u>, that ye withdraw yourselves from every brother that walketh disorderly, and not after the tradition which he received of us" (2 Thessalonians 3:6.)

The same 'method' is also used to mangle 2 Thessalonians 3:11,12: "For we hear that there are some which walk among you disorderly, working not at all, but are busybodies. Now them that are such we command and exhort <u>by our Lord Jesus Christ</u>, *that* with quietness they work, and eat their own bread."
This is not genuine Christian behaviour, neither should it ever be accepted as such.

"When Masonry mutilates the Holy Scripture by deliberately omitting the name of the Messiah it is no longer the God-breathed, inspired word of God. It is religion without Jesus Christ as Saviour and Redeemer."

This statement by the late Jim McCormick, himself an astute observer and writer of numerous articles on freemasonry over the years, is confirmed by Albert Pike in his lexicon of freemasonry. He writes: "A Christian Mason is not permitted to introduce his own peculiar opinions with regard to Christ's mediatorial office into the lodge."

It is interesting that in The Builder, a well-known Masonic book, there is no entry in the index for Jesus or Christ.

In Coils Masonic Encyclopaedia no such entry is listed either. Neither does Holman's Masonic Bible include an entry for either Jesus or Christ.

So I have to ask, does this not show the scornful attitude of any lodge toward Christianity? All prayers in the lodge it seems are Christ-less. How sad and how worthless.

So where does that leave the professing Christian as regards to worship in the lodge? Assuming he has got this far. Well, he can use the volume of the Sacred Law (VSL), Vedas, or the Gita. He can choose Zoroaster or the angelus for inspiration, if he so wishes. He can worship in any lodge behind closed doors in Trafalgar Square, off Broadway or near the Neverland Ranch (if he should wish to).

Yet did not Jesus proclaim: "For there is no man that doeth any thing in secret, and he himself seeketh to be known openly. If thou do these things, shew thyself to the world" (John 7:4).
And He also said the following: "I am the way, the truth, and the life: no man cometh unto the Father, but by me" (John 14:6).

So, what is going on here, I have to ask? And don't be taken in by the 'all seeing eye,' familiar in the lodge, and in nearly every music pop video too, not to mention on the back of a dollar bill. It is not the eye of God as Freemasons ignorantly claim but rather: "The all seeing eye (that) was the symbol of deity in the ancient mysteries of Egypt."

Secretism, it seems, announces another route, another door, independent of the Lord Jesus Christ. This I will not accept! Christ is not on par with Muhammad, Buddha, Confucius, Joseph Smith, Sitting Bull or any pope.

Freemasonry also states that: "If you deserve and purchase your path to heaven you are being saved by your own works, not God's works."

This is from the Freemasons Pocket Companion. The true Bible believing Christian knows that good works can never save you. Only real faith in the precious blood of Jesus Christ can achieve this. Nothing else. And if it did, what was the point of the crucifixion?

"He that is of God heareth God's words: ye therefore hear *them* not, because ye are not of God." (John 8:47).

So why are certain young and ambitious men and women attracted into becoming Freemasons?

In the Masonic catechism the novice is asked: "Why did you become a freemason?" "To obtain a knowledge of the secrets and mysteries preserved amongst the brethren."

In the world of business and commerce, it can offer promotion and in bringing in new business to the firm if a man is approached to join the lodge. This is very much a sweetener as well as the colourful regalia. And don't all men love a uniform and the whiff of secret societies. (For the purpose of this article and for the lack of space, I have excluded the Illuminati the Trilateral group, the Bilderbergers and other assorted anti-Christian institutions).

It must also be stated how many protestant ministers, elders, deacons, and Sunday school teachers, have all requested a place in the lodge. And shame on them!

Freemasonry rites are idolatry. This is clearly witnessed in the initiation oaths, especially in the first three degrees. Even God is re-named 'The Great Architect of the Universe!' Masons will not find Him in 'the grand lodge' in the sky! Rather they will meet the one true God at the Great White Throne Judgment if they do not renounce this movement and receive Christ as their only hope of salvation (Revelation 20:11-14.)

The apostle Paul was correct when he warned those seeking the truth not to be yoked with those who practice such acts (2 Corinthians 6:14-18.)
And did not Jesus warn: "Swear not at all" (Matthew 5:34).

In the ninetieth degree of the thirty-three degrees

of Freemasonry, the candidate is marked with balm with the words said over him: "Thou art a priest forever, after the order of Melchizedek."

The Bible believer must see this as blasphemy and unacceptable, not to mention that this office is non-transferable. It only belongs to Jesus Christ.

Incidentally, in the same degree (ninetieth) the candidate is presented with a sash embroidered with the 12 signs of the Zodiac. The Bible clearly forbids this divination (Deuteronomy 18:10-14). Again the true Bible believer should and must reject such a practice if it is offered to them.

And what about secret hand grips and mumbled oaths muttered in the dark. The apostle James gave the following warning on this: "But above all things, my brethren, swear not, neither by heaven, neither by the earth, neither by any other oath: but let your yea be yea; and your nay, nay; lest ye fall into condemnation" (James 5:12).

However for the mostly naïve and ignorant apprentice, he is starkly warned that his throat will be cut, his tongue and heart will be torn out and his discarded body will be marked and disembowelled, if any lodge secrets are revealed to non-masons!

So why would any sane person in his right frame of mind want to go along with this malarkey? One more thing a Christian should look out for are masonic rings, cuff links and tie clips, as well as fleece-lined aprons and silk, festooned ties, crystal glass or pewter decanters.

So my final advice to any ignorant Christian who may have joined Freemasonry is to repent and get out of it. Burn the regalia, don't wait. And if you've got children or grandchildren they'll love to assist you in stoking that fire in the garden. Perhaps your wife will also be very glad of your decision.

Remember what the apostle Paul wrote in 2 Corinthians 6:17: "Come ye out from among them," he later qualifies this in Ephesians 5:11: "Have no fellowship with the unfruitful works of darkness but rather reprove them. For it is a shame even to speak of those things which are done of them in secret."

So what more encouragement do you need?

May I once more quote the following source, which I believe sums up the sheer apostasy in Christendom today: "Freemasonry, far from declining, has been spreading. Most alarming, perhaps, is its penetration deep and wide into the established 'reformed' churches and the new ground it is breaking in the Evangelical fellowships of this and other lands" (ref. 2, p. 16).

So, not only has freemasonry infiltrated some of the reformed churches but according to Adam Weishaupt, the former Jesuit-trained Illuminati high priest: "The most wonderful thing of all is that the distinguished Lutheran and Calvinist theologians who belong to our order really believe that they see in it (Illuminati) the true and genuine sense of Christian religion. Oh, mortal man, is there anything you cannot be made to believe?"

May I suggest that those who are in reformed churches, or any church system for that matter, should start asking their pastors and elders whether any of them are practising freemasons or members of the Illuminati? If the answer comes back yes, may I suggest they run to the nearest exit? If this answer is no, ask them why they do not preach against such. And this would have to include all denominations for that matter, for we know that the Vineyard and Southern Baptists have Masonic pastors and elders too!

The apostle Paul warned believers to never be yoked to unsaved people: "Be ye not unequally yoked together with unbelievers: for what fellowship hath righteousness with unrighteousness? and what communion hath light with darkness? And what concord hath Christ with Belial? or what part hath he that believeth with an infidel? And what agreement hath the temple of God with idols? for ye are the temple of the living God; as God hath said, I will dwell in them, and walk in them; and I will be their God, and they shall be my people. Wherefore come out from among them, and be ye separate, saith the Lord, and touch not the unclean thing; and I will receive you, And will be a Father unto you, and ye shall be my sons and daughters, saith the Lord Almighty" (2 Corinthians 6:14-18).

The one thing all these groups have in common is how they are trying in vain to reach God or their god on their own terms and in their own ways. This is no different to what happened at Babel, and God was not interested in their approach then, and He certainly is not interested now (Genesis 11:4).

If a person wants to receive Jesus Christ as their Lord and Saviour and true light of the world, all they need to do is turn to Him in faith and trust in Him totally to forgive and save them. The Bible calls this repentance.

Disclaimer: citing the following sources for this

book is in no way an endorsement of such. They were simply consulted due to being experts on this subject.

Sources

Ref. 1: www.masonicinfo.com/pike.htm

Ref. 2: Christ, The Christian & Freemasonry, 1984, W. J. Mck. McCormick

Ref. 3: Is Freemasonry Christian, 1987, W. J. Mck McCormick

Ref. 4: What They Believe – *Masons*, 1990, Harold J. Berry

Ref. 5: The Light Bringers – *the truth about freemasonry*, DVD, 2005

Ref. 6: www.saintsalive.com (Ed Decker)

Ref. 7: The Facts on the Masonic Lodge, 1989, John Ankerberg and John Weldon

Ref. 8: Secret Societies, 1983, George L. Hunt

Ref. 9: The Truth Uncovered, DVD, 2004

Ref. 10: Born in the Blood – The Lost Secrets of Freemasonry, 1989, John J. Robinson

Ref. 11: Masonry – Beyond the Light, 1991, William Schnoebelen

Ref. 12: Behind Closed Doors, 1999, W. P. Malcomson

Ref. 13: The Secret Societies Handbook, 2005, Michael Bradley

Ref. 14: Masonic Lodge, Texe Marrs, DVD

Ref. 15: Inside the Brotherhood, 1989, Martin Short

Ref. 16: Character and Claims of Freemasonry, 1889, Charles G. Finney

I must also credit two books by Barry Smith Second Warning and How To Set A Freemason Free, Harold J. Berry's What They Believe: Masons, and William Harvey The Complete Manual of Freemasonry.

ABOUT THE AUTHOR

James G. Battell

James G. Battell is a Christian writer, radio broadcaster, video maker, and podcaster. He also runs an international Bible-believing ministry with his father (www.excatholicsforchrist.com).

Printed in Great Britain
by Amazon